Contents

Any words appearing in the text in bold, **like this**, are explained in the glossary. You can also look out for them in the Word bank at the bottom of each page.

Young crime

Giving dad a hand

The Code of Hammurabi is an ancient set of laws about crime, trade, and family life. Punishments for breaking the laws depended on the wealth and power of the **offender**, or the details of the crime. The less power an offender had, the worse punishment he was likely to receive.

"Youth opens fire on schoolyard".

"Youth gang shoots girls dead".

"Kids out of control".

Newspaper headlines like these can make us believe that young people are now causing more crime than ever before. But is that really true? Are young people today more likely to be **criminals** than in the past?

A look back through history soon shows that young people have always been involved in crimes – and punished for them. Sometimes young people were punished even when they had done very little wrong. Many full-time criminals began their lives of crime when they were young.

It was written in the Code of Hammurabi that if a son ever hit his father, he would have his hand chopped off. ⁘⋯

Teenage crime is nothing new – it has been going on for centuries. ⋯⁘

criminal   anyone who breaks the law

A Painful History of Childhood

Fiendish Crimes
and
Punishing Times

John Townsend

www.raintreepublishers.co.uk
Visit our website to find out more information about **Raintree** books.

To order:
☎ Phone 44 (0) 1865 888112
▤ Send a fax to 44 (0) 1865 314091
▢ Visit the Raintree Bookshop at www.raintreepublishers.co.uk to browse our catalogue and order online.

First published in Great Britain by Raintree,
Halley Court, Jordan Hill, Oxford OX2 8EJ,
part of Harcourt Education.
Raintree is a registered trademark of
Harcourt Education Ltd.

© Harcourt Education Ltd 2006
First published in paperback in 2007
The moral right of the proprietor has
been asserted.

Editorial: Melanie Waldron and Lucy Beevor
Design: Philippa Jenkins and Q2A
Illustrations: Q2A
Picture Research: Mica Brancic and Elaine Willis
Production: Chloe Bloom

Originated by Modern Age
Printed and bound in China by South China
Printing Company

10 digit ISBN 1 406 20079 4 (hardback)
13 digit ISBN 978 1 406 20079 9

10 digit ISBN 1 406 20086 7 (paperback)
13 digit ISBN 978 1 406 20086 7

11 10 09 08 07
10 9 8 7 6 5 4 3 2 1

**British Library Cataloguing in
Publication Data**
Townsend, John
Fiendish crimes and punishing times. –
(A painful history of childhood)
364'.09
A full catalogue record for this book is
available from the British Library.

Acknowledgements
AKG-images pp. 10–11 (Erich Lessing); Bridgeman
Art Library p. 14 (Stapleton Collection); Chicago
Historical Society pp. 24–25, 25; Corbis pp. 6–7,
16–17, 18, 22–23, 24, 26–27; Corbis pp. 5(t), 10,
12, 18–19, 19, 27 (Bettmann), 12–13 (D. S. Cole),
36 (David Butow), 7 (David Samuel Robbins), 42
(Don Mason), 43 (Gabe Palmer), 26 (Hulton-
Deutsch Collection), 41 (In Visu/Jerome Sessini),
23 (Jacob August Riis), 29 (James Noble), 28 (John
B. Boykin), 5(m) and 9 (Kevin Fleming), 34–35
(Peter Turnley), 16 (Photo Collection Alexander
Alland, Sr.), title and 5 (Robert Essel NYC), 30–31
(Shelley Gazin); Getty pp. 32–33, 8–9 (Hulton
Archive); Mary Evans Picture Library pp. 6, 14–15,
20–21, 28–29; National Archvies UK p. 20; Rex
Features pp. 42–43 (Alix/Phanie), 33 (Bob
Crandall), 5(b) and 38 (Chris Eads), 4 (Image
Source), 38–39 (Jeremy Sutton Hibbert), 36–37
(John Powell), 40–41 (Raphael Cardinael), 34, 37
(Sipa Press), 39 (Stuart Clarke); State Library of
Tasmania p. 15 (Heritage Collection); The Kobal
Collection pp. 40 (Dreamworks/Andrew Cooper),
30 (Goldwyn/United Artists).

Cover photograph of young boys staring out from
Newgate prison door, reproduced with permission of
Getty/Hulton Archive.

The publishers would like to thank Bill Marriott for
his assistance in the preparation of this book.

Every effort has been made to contact copyright
holders of any material reproduced in this book.
Any omissions will be rectified in subsequent
printings if notice is given to the publishers.

Nothing new

Ever since the first laws were made thousands of years ago, some people have set out to break them. Many of these criminals have been young.

- Sometimes they knew no better.
- Sometimes they were just doing as they were told by older criminals or parents.
- Sometimes they had no choice if they were to survive.

Youth crime is nothing new. It was mentioned in a set of laws called the Code of Hammurabi, written in Babylon (now Iraq), nearly 4,000 years ago. These laws were made to protect the weak from violent attacks. Sometimes the attackers were young criminals.

Find out later ...

Who killed 21 people in the 1850s?

What punishment might you receive for cutting down a tree?

How do electronic tags stop crime?

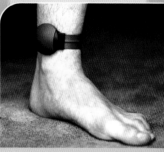

offender   person who commits a crime

From the earliest times, young people have often got into trouble. It usually comes with growing up, taking risks, and making mistakes.

Juvenile crime was part of life in most ancient civilizations, such as in Greece and Rome. For hundreds of years afterwards, young **criminals** were punished just like adults. All criminals were treated the same, whatever their age. In many countries children as young as seven were put on **trial** and punished just like anyone else. That often meant being **hanged**. It is only in the last 300 years that detailed criminal records have been kept, which show that juvenile crime is certainly nothing new.

A police officer leads richer people through the **slums** of Five Points in New York. ⋯⋯▸

hanging   practice of killing criminals by hanging them with a rope around the neck

Turning to crime

Crime has always been a problem. Although most crimes are carried out by adults, this book is about crimes committed by juveniles.

Around 300 years ago towns and cities in Europe and the United States were growing quickly. People were moving to the towns and cities from the countryside to find better jobs. City streets were crowded, and more people meant more rich pickings for thieves.

In the 1700s very few children went to school. Many children grew up unable to read or write. Unskilled people could only get jobs that paid very poorly. For many, the temptation to turn to crime to get more money was just too great.

The rope that was used to hang people was called a noose.

She knew no better

Elizabeth Marsh, aged fifteen, was hanged for the murder of her grandfather at Dorchester, United Kingdom, in 1794. She had given him two blows to his head as he slept. The judge said she had been brought up not knowing right from wrong, or the difference between good and evil.

juvenile   young person who is not quite an adult
trial   hearing and judgment of a case in court

30 July, 1730

A gang of 30 pick-pocket boys, who rob in Covent Garden each night, were caught by the watchmen. Eight of the boys were sent to do **hard labour** in Bridewell Prison. The oldest was not more than thirteen, and most of them swore in a dreadful manner.

Life on the street

In the 1700s, there were many homeless children in cities. They were either thrown out into the streets by uncaring parents, or they were **orphaned** because of diseases that killed many people at that time.

Living rough on the streets with nowhere to go, nothing to do, and nothing to eat often led young people to get into crime. In the 1700s there were no proper police forces, so turning to crime seemed an easy choice. Older **criminals** were on the look-out to **enlist** children into gangs of thieves. After all, the smaller the thieves, the narrower the gaps they could squeeze through to steal things!

First police

Many city leaders wanted to do something to stop the rise in street crime and young pick-pocket gangs in the mid-1700s. They organized street **patrols**.

King George III is ⋯⋗ protected by the Bow Street Runners, in the late 1700s.

Word bank

enlist get someone to join in, or get their support
orphan young person whose parents are dead

Watchmen patrolled the streets trying to find young robbers at work.

In New York in the 1700s watchmen carried wooden rattles to make a loud alarm if they witnessed a crime. This was to call for help to catch the criminal.

In London, the first group of paid policemen began to patrol the streets in the 1750s. Their base was in Bow Street, and so they were called Bow Street Runners. They were the first proper police force to begin to tackle street crime.

Can you imagine anyone being sentenced to death for cutting a tree down today?

Did you know?

- By the end of the 1700s, the US prison system kept all young criminals in cells with adult prisoners.
- In the 1700s, over 200 crimes were punishable by death in the United Kingdom – whatever a person's age. That included stealing, cutting down a tree, or **poaching** a rabbit.

patrol watch over an area
poach illegally hunt or catch animals on private property

Punishment

People thought that if young people were punished for their crimes, they would never break the law again. It would also show other young people that crime did not pay. However, this idea did not always work. Even very young children sometimes **offended** again and again.

Throughout US history, there have been long debates about when children were old enough to be held responsible for their actions. Laws in the late 1700s said that any child over the age of seven should be punished just the same as adults. That meant children were sent to adult prisons, or even put to death if they were found guilty of serious crimes.

Did you know?

In the 1700s any child under the age of seven who committed a crime in the United States could not be **prosecuted**. But any child committing a crime after their seventh birthday could be sent to a prison such as Greenwich State Prison (below). This was New York's first state prison, which opened in 1787.

Word bank   convict   find or prove a person is guilty
death penalty   punishment by death

Prison

Locking up children with adult criminals was the worst way to punish them. They soon learned far more about crime from the older experts! In the 1700s prisons were filthy and violent places. Prisoners were badly fed and often beaten. Many people argued that locking up young **criminals** in such bad conditions only made them behave worse.

Even in the 1700s some people felt that the **death penalty** was not the best way to prevent crime. In fact, because punishments were so harsh, **juries** often refused to **convict** younger people. As a result, many teenagers were set free to carry on breaking the law.

Death

Some US states in the late 1700s discussed getting rid of the death penalty altogether. In 1794 Pennsylvania stopped the death penalty for all crimes, apart from murder. In time, many other states did the same.

Scene at court, from 1710, shows the terrible conditions awaiting young criminals sent to prison.

jury   group of people in a court that decides if someone is guilty or not

In the 1800s people began to change their minds about how to treat young **criminals**. Was it right for young people to be locked up in prison? Was it right for people to rush to public **hangings** to watch children being put to death? Crowds would cheer when the rope was put around the criminal's neck and the body swung from the **gallows**.

The death penalty

In Maidstone, United Kingdom, a nine-year-old boy was **sentenced** to death in 1833 for stealing. There was a public outcry. People thought this punishment was wrong – so he was allowed to live. Public opinion was beginning to make a difference.

People were led to **execution** for all sorts of crimes.

Word bank   **gallows**   wooden structure used for hanging a person
sentence   punishment set by a court

Hanging

James Guild was twelve years old when he killed an old woman in New Jersey, United States, in 1827. He had learning difficulties, and did not seem to understand what he had done. Newspapers told how he played with mice in his cell just before he was hanged.

Thousands of people went to watch James Guild's hanging. As the trapdoor fell away beneath him and the rope tightened around his neck, James put his toes on the edge of the trapdoor to save himself. A **sheriff** knocked his feet from the edge, and James dropped into the hole and died. Incidents like this shocked many people.

Public hangings, like this one in Missouri, United States, were seen as a warning to others: crime leads to death. ❖...

sheriff   official of an area who is in charge of enforcing the law

Child convicts

From 1788 to 1868, the UK Government came up with a new way to get rid of many prisoners. It was called **transportation**. In 80 years around 160,000 convicts were sent from the United Kingdom to Australia, over 12,000 miles away.

After being locked up in filthy ships that took months to reach Australia, the **convicts** had to work for years, often in chains. Many prisoners died on the journey, including children. Some of the children were convicts themselves, while others went to be with their convicted parents.

Terrible conditions

Any **criminal** over seven years old could be chained up and locked in a cage on board a convict ship. They were often **flogged**, and many died from disease or bad food. Storms at sea and sea-sickness could make the journey grim for young convicts.

The people on the first convict ships did not know whether they would ever see their families again.

Convicts were sometimes locked up in cages to stop any trouble onboard the ship.

Word bank   **flogged**   beaten severely with a rod or whip

Never to return

Robert Haybard was nine years old in 1843 when he was convicted of stealing a pot of beef. He was put on a ship bound for Australia.

When Robert Haybard arrived in Australia, he was among the lucky ones. He was given training to learn a trade instead of being put in prison or forced to do **hard labour** building roads. In time he was able to live like other settlers.

Many convict ships sank. This is the wreck of the *Waterloo*, which sank in August 1842.

Lost

The *Amphitrite* was a convict ship. In August 1833 it sailed from London, United Kingdom, with 106 female convicts and 12 children on board. It was wrecked on rocks soon after setting sail. It was the first convict ship to sink. There were only three survivors.

transportation sending criminals far away to another country

Houses of refuge

During the early 1800s many young **offenders** on US streets were taken away to "houses of **refuge**". These were safe places where offenders were kept secure and sheltered from the risks of street life. In a refuge they would learn – through hard work and rules – how to become a good citizen. Any young person could be made to stay in a house of refuge by the police. They were secure homes where the **inmates** had to stay until they were over eighteen – usually until they were twenty-one.

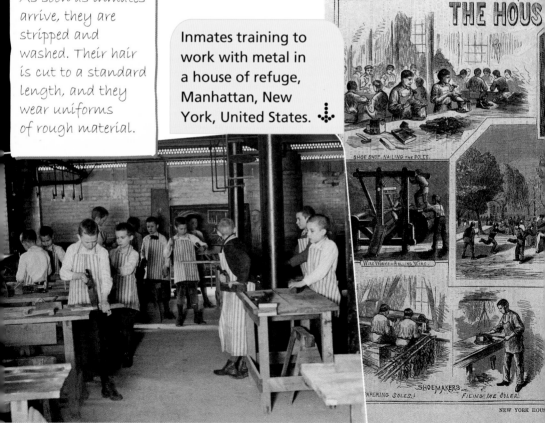

Inmates training to work with metal in a house of refuge, Manhattan, New York, United States.

SHOE SHOP - NAILING THE SOLES.

THE HOUS

WIRE WORKS - ROLLING WIRE.

SHOEMAKERS

PERING SOLES.

FILING THE SOLES.

NEW YORK HOUS

Word bank

asylum place of safety
reform correct or improve behaviour or habits

Life inside

Houses of refuge were sometimes called **asylums**. They were supposed to be "safe havens" to protect the young from the evils of the outside world. In fact, many houses of refuge were just like prisons. Each hall could hold up to 200 narrow cells. Windows were often tiny and barred, and doors were made of heavy iron.

A bell rang to wake the inmates and to signal meal times. If anyone broke the rules, he or she spent days alone in a cell with just bread and water. They were forced to sit with one foot chained to a heavy iron ball, and were whipped.

Different approach

The houses of refuge of the early 1800s just did not work. Young people soon offended again once they got back on the streets. The United States opened **reform** schools instead. One of the first to open was in Ohio, in 1858. The idea was that ten to eighteen-year-old boys should be treated more like pupils than prisoners.

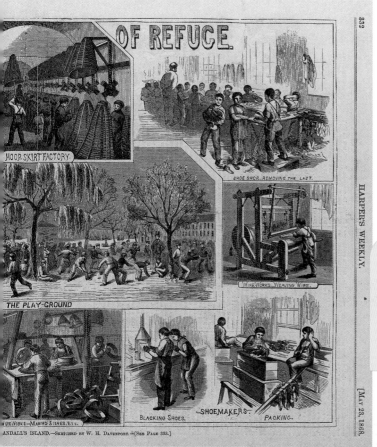

The House of Refuge by W. H. Davenport, 1868, shows scenes from the New York house of refuge on Randall's Island.

refuge   place that provides shelter or protection

Rising street crime

On the move

From 1840 to 1860 more immigrants than ever arrived in the United States. Most were from Europe. During the Irish potato **famine** (below), from 1845 to 1851, there was nothing left to eat. Many hungry people arrived in the United States looking for food and work. By 1860, one in every four people in New York City had been born in Ireland.

Throughout the 1800s US towns and cities grew faster than ever before. More and more people arrived from **rural** areas or from other countries. Industry was booming, and there was money to be made in the cities. Some people who worked in factories now earned good wages. **Criminals** soon started to prowl the rich city streets.

At risk

Some cities in the United States had major crime problems, as young robber-gangs took to the streets. Rich people wearing watches and jewels, or with silk handkerchiefs and full purses, were easy **prey** for young street criminals.

immigrant   someone who comes to live permanently in a foreign country

Growing trouble

Immigrants who arrived in the United States believed they would find a better life in "the New World". However, there were not enough houses or jobs for everyone, and many immigrants had to live crowded together in **slums**. Their children often begged in the streets or found money in other ways. Some of these children ended up in gangs. Groups of young thieves and vandals roamed the streets of New York, Boston, and other cities.

For many immigrants, life was worse when they arrived in the United States.

The Wild West

From the mid-1800s people **migrated** west across the United States. They settled in small towns in wild countryside in what became called the Wild West. This was also **bandit** country. Some of the bandits were young, like Billy the Kid (above). Born in the 1850s, he is reported to have killed 21 men, one for each year of his life. In fact, he may only have killed nine people – but that is still nine too many!

prey   person who is helpless, or unable to escape attack

Young criminals

In the 1800s the writer Charles Dickens was shocked by the level of street crime in the smoky, filthy cities of the United Kingdom. He knew about the gangs of young pickpockets that were run by cruel adults. The pickpockets often had to work like slaves for their ring-leaders. Anything they stole had to be given to their "owner". In return they would be given scraps of food and shelter for the night.

Charles Dicken's book *Oliver Twist*, published in 1838, was about a gang of pickpockets run by an evil ring-leader called Fagin. It was set in London, but it could have been any big city at that time.

20 Word bank   **reformatory**   place similar to a prison, where the aim is to change the bad behaviour of young criminals

School or prison?

When young pickpockets were caught, nobody knew what to do with them. Sending them to adult prisons or for **transportation** was now seen as wrong. It was time to try something new.

One idea was **reformatory** schools. These were similar to prisons, but instead the aim was to change, or reform, a young person's bad behaviour. Inmates could stay for several years in these schools. Those who misbehaved were whipped and made to spend a few days in an unheated cell with just bread and water.

Reformatory schools

In the late 1800s more reformatory schools were tried in the United States. Many ended up being just like real prisons, with as many as 500 young people in a cellblock. Parents were even known to arrive at the gates to turn over their unruly children, demanding they were punished!

A scene from the 2005 movie *Oliver Twist* shows Fagin and Oliver preparing for a night of pick-pocketing.

New York

By the 1850s, New York had over half a million people and had set up its own police force. The city had more problems than others because so many homeless **immigrants** kept arriving each day. There were often fights between different groups of immigrants. In the **slum** areas of the Lower East Side and Five Points, crime rates soared because of overcrowding, unemployment, and gang fights.

Young pickpockets in the streets were given all kinds of names like "rats", "gamins", "urchins", and "gutter-snipes." Most of these **criminals** were between ten and seventeen years old.

Homeless

In the 1850s there were about 10,000 homeless young people living on the streets of New York. The new city police force began to round up thousands of homeless young criminals each year. Before long, over 1,000 teens up to the age of fifteen were sent to prison each year for various street crimes.

Men from opposing gangs fight in the Five Points area of New York, 1827.

Word bank

court   group of people before whom legal cases are heard
deter   discourage someone acting in a particular way

Young pickpockets

By the 1870s, the New York Police had a fight on their hands to catch hundreds of teenage pickpockets. The **courts** began to give tough prison **sentences** to **deter** others from street crime. Judges even sent young pickpockets to the dreaded Sing Sing Jail to teach them a harsh lesson.

It was during this time that teenagers John Golden and Alfred Johnson were **convicted** of pick-pocketing just 28 pence. They each received 3-year prison sentences as a warning to others. In the mid-1870s New York's judges convicted almost 10,000 teenagers a year. Many of them were under fourteen years old.

Gangs of New York

Many of New York's young homeless people in the 1870s slept rough among factories, brickyards, docks, and railroad yards. Many lived in an area called Hell's Kitchen where the city **slaughterhouses** were. One street called 11th Avenue had the nickname "Death Avenue" because of the fights between violent gangs of young criminals.

Loitering in the streets of New York, 1888. ••••

slaughterhouse   place where animals are slaughtered for food

New ways

Catching young **offenders** on US city streets was a big task throughout the 1800s. But the old problem of dealing with so many **criminals** after they were caught was hard to solve.

As early as 1841 a Boston shoemaker called John Augustus came up with an idea. He persuaded the police to release young **convicts**, and said that he would try to help them change their behaviour. Then he kept visiting them at home to make sure they were not breaking the law. This was an early form of **probation** support. It was carried on by **volunteers** until about 1899, when many US states first paid for full-time probation officers.

Juvenile courts appeared all over the United States during the early 1900s. Here, three boys sit in the Juvenile Court Chambers of Denver, Colorado. •••

probation   period of time when a prisoner is released, but his or her behaviour is supervised

Courts for juveniles

The first **juvenile** court, a special court where young people went on **trial**, was set up in Chicago in 1899. By 1925, nearly all states in the US had juvenile courts. They said they looked after the "best interests of the child", because they used judges who were specially trained to deal with young people. Smaller rooms were used instead of big, unfriendly courtrooms. Also, juvenile cases were not open to the public like adult trials, so they were private and less frightening.

Whenever possible, the main punishment given by the juvenile court was probation rather than a **sentence** in a young offenders' prison.

From (left to right): judges Frank Johnston, Jr., Jesse A. Baldwin, and John P. McGoonty in a courtroom in Chicago, Illinois, 1919.

The first juvenile court, Chicago, 1907.

Ground-breaking

In the early 1900s, Judge Julian Mack of Chicago told the juvenile court judge:

"Do not decide if a boy or girl committed a wrong . . . but do decide what had best be done in his or her interest to save him or her from a downward career."

This was a very new way of thinking!

volunteer someone who offers to do a job without being paid

1900s — Fighting back

The 1900s was a century of great change in fighting the problem of **juvenile** crime. Some of the new ideas for change have involved:

- Improving the **slums** and bad conditions where many young people were growing up.
- Educating and training young people so that they could find worthwhile jobs, to prevent them turning to crime.
- Using the period of punishment in a positive way to train **convicted criminals** and give them skills to use for useful work.
- Giving support and guidance to people released from **detention** centres.

Borstals

In the United Kingdom reform schools were known as Borstals, after a place in Kent where they began in 1902. They were run more like boarding schools with a lot of sport and skills training. The staff did not wear uniforms. Borstals ran like this for the next 80 years, when they were replaced with Y.O.I.s, or Youth Offender Institutions.

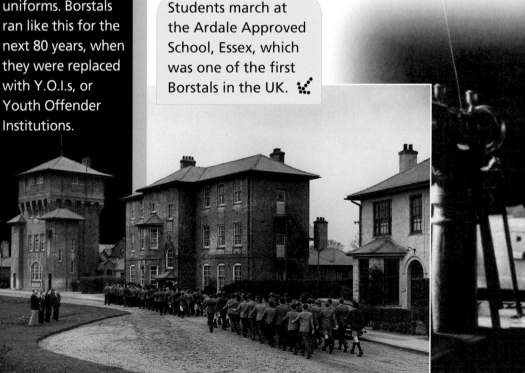

Students march at the Ardale Approved School, Essex, which was one of the first Borstals in the UK.

Word bank   **detention**   punishment of being kept inside a secure place

Tackling the cause

People began to recognise that there was often a link between a troubled home life, an unhappy childhood, and teenage crime. Soon, breaking the law was seen not so much as evil or as a major weakness in a person, but as a possible result of a bad upbringing. By giving criminals a better chance in life, perhaps they could change.

The old **reform** schools of the 1800s began to be run in new ways. **Inmates** were taught trades such as carpentry or tailoring. They lived in groups in houses with a live-in "house-parent". The new schools hoped to improve the behaviour of young criminals by treating them in a more civilised way.

A new approach

The Oregon State Reform School opened in Salem in 1891, but within 20 years it had become the State Training School for Boys. Boys stayed there for 1 or 2 years learning in the workshops (above), steam laundry, kitchen, blacksmiths, and barbershop.

Sixteen-year-old Charles Nichols makes shoes in the workshop at Colorado Reform School, United States, 1920.

inmate person kept in prison

Would you prefer
to be locked up in
prison for several
years, or have your
sentence cut to just
6 months at a boot
camp? But there
would be a small
price to pay. You
would have to:

- get up very early.
- go on long
  marches in
  heavy boots.
- run miles
  every day.
- do a lot of
  hard labour.
- get shouted
  at by a "drill
  sergeant".

Short, sharp shock

At the same time that many **reformatory** schools
were trying to show a more caring approach,
other ideas were being put to the test.

From the 1940s the California Youth Authority
began a programme for young **criminals** that was
run in the style of strict military training. This
included shouting at young **offenders**, making
them run miles wearing heavy back-packs, and
giving them tough **discipline**. Drill instructors
tried to bully offenders into good behaviour.
New York State's Elmira Reformatory tried
long days of exercise and marching with wooden
rifles. Before long, camps like this came to an
end as they just did not seem to work.

Boot camps can
sometimes be
tougher than a
stay in prison. ➽

Boot camps

The short, sharp shock approach returned in the United States in the late 1970s. In 1974 Idaho started a 4-month programme for young offenders on an old Air Force base. They became known as "boot camps" as they involved a lot of marching, like soldiers, in heavy boots. Around 10 years later Georgia and Oklahoma opened more boot camps.

With public outrage at growing youth crime rates, more boot camps were set up in the 1980s and 1990s in the United States. Thousands of young offenders faced 6 months of hard work and hard exercise. They still do in many boot camps across the US!

How would you cope marching in these heavy boots all day?

Did you know?

In the mid-1990s about 30 states across the United States had boot camps for first-time, non-violent, young **offenders**. Almost 9,000 thirteen to seventeen- year-olds were given long days of hard work in an attempt to make them respect authority. Those who failed were sent back to **juvenile court** for a judge to decide their next course of punishment.

Dealing with young offenders

The idea that it was the responsibility of the whole community to care for troubled young people developed in the 1900s. Rather than punish every **criminal** in exactly the same way, a young person's background was taken into account more often. After all, many young criminals were often themselves victims of all kinds of **abuse**.

Courts started to believe that young people were far more likely to be saved from a life of crime than adults were. They thought that even the most badly behaved child could be trained with firm guidance and proper schooling.

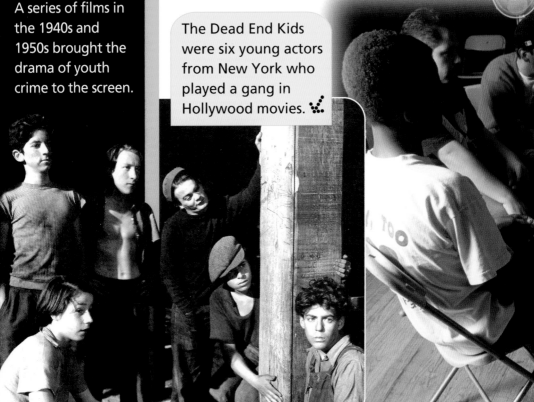

The Dead End Kids were six young actors from New York who played a gang in Hollywood movies.

abuse to hurt or injure through ill treatment

New laws

Throughout the 1900s both Europe and the United States started to see that troubled teenagers, as well as their parents, often needed help and support rather than just punishment. Laws began to change to stop very young criminals being punished as harshly as they used to be.

In 1908 the United Kingdom changed the law so that nobody younger than sixteen could be hanged, and nobody under fourteen could be sent to adult prisons. It took another 80 years before the United States banned the **death penalty** for murderers aged sixteen or below.

Teenagers who get into trouble join support groups to talk through their problems.

Criminals or victims?

A 2003 study at Edinburgh University, Scotland, found that young offenders have often been victims of crime themselves. If an offender had been a victim of crime by the age of twelve, they were more likely to offend by the age of fifteen. Also, those who offended at twelve were more likely to become victims of crime by the age of fifteen.

Young killers

In 1978 a fifteen-year-old boy called Willie Bosket caused the law in New York to be changed. Bosket had committed over 2,000 crimes by the time he was fifteen. His father was a **convicted** murderer, and Willie had killed two people just "to see what it felt like". People felt his crimes were too serious for the **Juvenile Court,** so the law was changed.

The new Juvenile **Offender** Act of 1978 was known as the "Willie Bosket law". Now violent juveniles like Bosket can be tried in adult courts – just as they have been through history. This law makes sure that young killers can be sent to prison for life.

Teen killers

During the early 1980s around 1,000 murders were committed by teens each year in the United States. By the middle of the 1990s, this had grown to over 3,000 per year, or almost 10 percent of all murders.

A US police officer **patrols** a New York subway train in the 1970s.

Word bank   executed be put to death for a crime

Willie Bosket caught on the subway

Willie Bosket rode the New York subways looking for someone to rob. He had been in and out of court since he was nine. But he knew the Juvenile Court did not have the power to send him to an adult prison.

Willie found himself alone with another rider on a train. He took out his gun and killed the man. Even if he got caught, he knew the law could not stop him. However, he was soon arrested and the law was quickly changed to make sure he went to prison in 1978, never to be freed.

Another law change

In 1988 the United States stopped the **death penalty** for all offenders under the age of sixteen. The same year, seventeen-year-old Scott Hain was **sentenced** to death for killing two people. He was put to death in 2003 in Oklahoma City. Scott Hain was the last teenager under eighteen to be **executed** in the United States. In 2005 a new law banned the death penalty for all murderers under the age of eighteen.

The new laws state that juveniles under the age of eighteen cannot be executed, by electric chair or other means. ❖••••

Recent times, recent crimes

Did you know?

Serious violent crimes by juveniles occur most often in the hours straight after the close of school on school days. Most adult crime happens later at night.

Through history young people have often been blamed for causing more crime than they actually do. The cases that make the news can lead people to think that youth crime must be growing and is worse than ever.

In the last 20 years **juvenile** crime appears to have risen in many countries. But this growth in crime is only keeping pace with the growth of the population in these countries. Although there may be more **criminals** around than in the past, there are also far more law-abiding people around.

Is this a young criminal about to strike?

Recent trends

Crime figures must be looked at over many years to see if there are any real changes or trends. The reasons behind the figures are not always clear. In the United States, recent figures show some interesting signs:

- Violent crimes committed by young people changed little between 1973 and 1989.
- They reached an all-time high in 1993, but have fallen since by 47 percent.
- One of the reasons for this drop could be the arrests of many drug gangs in recent years.

Behind the figures

In Canada it seems that youth crime fell by 17 percent from 2002 to 2004. But that may not mean there were fewer crimes, just that fewer young people went to **court**. The reason for this fall may be the new Youth **Justice** Act, which sends fewer young people to court. Instead, juveniles are now given firm warnings for less serious crimes.

A juvenile is arrested in Los Angeles, United States.

Stay at home

Many people think that **juvenile** crime could be prevented if young people were kept off the streets. This is also the thinking behind many of the court orders for young **offenders** today.

For many years some areas have had laws called **curfews** to stop people below a certain age being out at certain times. Many curfews apply only to people under the age of eighteen, but sometimes in special circumstances there is no age limit.

A Los Angeles police officer advises a young boy about the city curfews, 1995.

It is illegal to damage public property with graffiti.

curfew   law requiring certain, or all, people to be off the streets at a stated time

Unfair?

Curfews actually date back hundreds of years, and they are still being used to prevent crime. Many towns across the United States have recently brought in curfew laws. Camden, New Jersey, has a curfew every 30 and 31 October to prevent Halloween pranks and possible crimes. Other towns have curfews during school hours to stop students missing class.

Young people who break a curfew may have to spend a few hours at the police station, or may be driven home by the police. Parents can be fined, or may even get a short jail **sentence**. Although curfews stop some young people getting into crime, they also punish **innocent** young people who also have to stay indoors.

Crime at home

Staying at home no longer means that crime is out of reach. Many teenagers have recently been **convicted** of **cyber crime**. This is any offence using a computer (above). Crimes can include **hacking** into another computer, writing a computer virus, or stealing information. All this can be done from home.

hack   gain access to a computer illegally
innocent   free from guilt or blame

Technology

Technology in the 21st century can make sure young **criminals** obey their **curfew** orders. By using **electronic tags** and CCTV cameras, the police can keep a close check on what **offenders** are doing.

In the United Kingdom **courts** punish some young criminals with an ASBO – an **antisocial** behaviour order. This order can ban a person from being at a particular place at a certain time. An electronic tag can show if someone breaks the order. That could lead to arrest and even a **sentence** at a young offenders' prison. From 2005 offenders as young as twelve were "tagged" in the United Kingdom.

Keeping track

Electronic collars were first used to help scientists track animals in the 1960s. Now the police can track people using an electronic unit attached to a bracelet. This can not be removed from an offender's ankle or wrist (below). The signal given by the "tag" can tell the police exactly where the offender is.

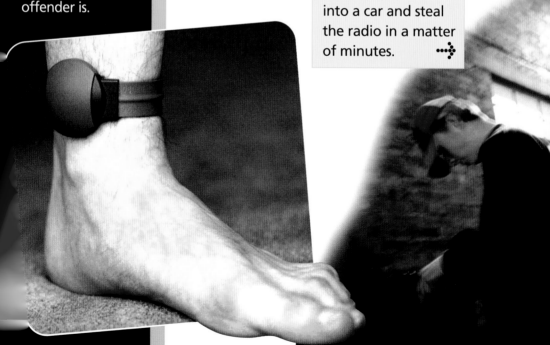

Gangs can break into a car and steal the radio in a matter of minutes. ⋯⋗

antisocial   bad for society and causing annoyance to others

Spy in the sky

The first electronic monitors in the United States were used in 1984. Within 6 years, over 65,000 offenders across the country were wearing electronic tags.

At one time, the person being monitored had to stay within range of a signal. Today satellite tracking can pinpoint exactly where an offender is at any time. Satellites as high as 17,702 kilometres (11,000 miles) above Earth can tell the police if a young offender has gone to school, is in a banned part of town, or is even committing another crime!

Many shopping malls now ban young people from wearing "hoodies" that hide their faces on CCTVs.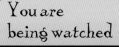

You are being watched

The gangs of young pickpockets that once robbed people in the streets would soon get caught today in many city centres and shopping malls. Now hundreds of CCTV cameras could be recording your every move as you walk through town. Many can zoom in very close and record every detail.

electronic tag   device attached to someone that sends a signal to show where they are

bagnale
youngest
o be on
list of the
wanted
Aged
1964,
me and
ging his
d the
shocking
vas
eonardo

m

You
right).

In the news

Crime stories are always in the news. The younger the **criminal**, the more shocking the story. In 2002 over 300 ten-year-olds were **convicted** of violent crimes in the United Kingdom. This is the youngest age that UK children can be **prosecuted** at today.

Armed robber, aged twelve (2004)

A twelve-year-old boy has held up a shop with a sawn-off shotgun in the West Midlands, United Kingdom. He is believed to be the UK's youngest armed robber. The boy was caught on CCTV video using a gun, which was not loaded. The boy was put on a **curfew** between 7 p.m. and 7 a.m. and must wear an **electronic tag**. He was too young to be sent to prison.

FBI United State's Federal Bureau of Investigation, which investigates serious crime

Getting the right picture

News stories about youth crime can lead the public to think of all young people as crime **suspects**! But they should check their figures. A US **juvenile** crime expert has said,

"Juveniles account for about 11 percent of all the arrests for violent crime. The public thinks they account for over 75 percent."

– Barry Krisberg, National Council for Crime and Delinquency (NCCD), United States.

Shoplifters are more often older people than teenagers.

Girl crime

The biggest difference in crime rates today compared with 100 years ago is the number of young females now committing crimes and being sent to prison (above). The most common **offence** is theft. But some girls are getting involved in fights and gang crime. Experts blame this trend on an increase in drinking, drug-taking, and on the pressures facing young girls today.

forge   make copies of items and pretend they are the real thing

A safer future?

Many teenagers have far more opportunities to commit crime today. 100 years ago they did not have the chance to even try car crime, drugs, **cyber crime**, or graffiti. Today young people tend to have more money than ever before, as well as more valuables such as watches, mobile phones, and trainers. Young people are now more likely to be the victims of other young people as they have far more belongings worth stealing.

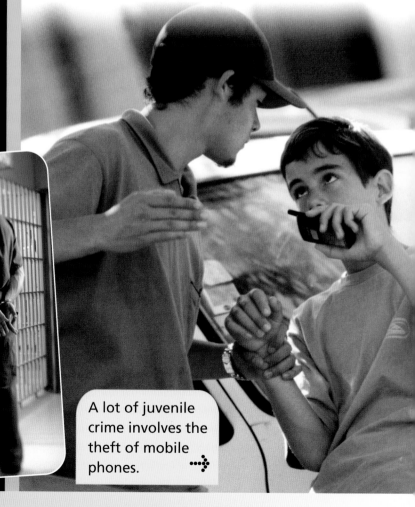

A lot of juvenile crime involves the theft of mobile phones.

Getting better?

Often the public fears that "the youth of today" are more **criminal** than ever before. Despite some shocking news stories that often give young people a bad name, there is hope...

Teens Behaving Better (2005)

Young people today are doing better than their parents. They take fewer drugs and commit fewer crimes. The number of youth **offenders** and victims has fallen since 1993 in the United States.

Twelve percent of youths aged twelve to seventeen were victims of crime in 1994. This fell to about 4.5 percent in 2004.

Crime on the decrease

A US study of "today's youth" has shown that, since 1993, young people have been engaging in less risky behaviour. That means they are committing fewer crimes.

66 With today's teens, maybe we have the next "greatest generation" coming along here. 99

– Jeffrey Butts, director of the Youth **Justice** Program at the Washington Urban Institute, 2005.

Many young people enjoy helping in the community, rather than harming it! ⋅⬦⋯

Find out more

Further reading

A Painful History of Crime: Crime Through Time, John Townsend (Raintree, 2005)

Crime and Detection, Brian Lane (DK Eyewitness Guides, 2005)

True Crime: Cops and Robbers, John Townsend (Raintree, 2004)

Using the Internet

Explore the Internet to find out more about childhood crime through the ages. You can use a search engine, such as **www.yahooligans.com**, and type in keywords such as:

- boot camps
- capital punishment
- cyber crime.

Search tips

There are billions of pages on the Internet so it can be difficult to find exactly what you are looking for.

These search tips will help you find useful websites more quickly:

- Know exactly what you want to find out about first.
- Use two to six keywords in a search, putting the most important words first.
- Be precise. Only use names of people, places, or things.

Australia

Just as in some other countries, Australia has had to punish fewer **juveniles** in the 21st century. The crime rate among juveniles fell by 20 percent between 2001 and 2003. In the same time, it fell by about 17 percent in the United States.

United States

In 2003 around 2.2 million **juveniles** were arrested for committing crimes. Juveniles were involved in:

- one in twelve arrests for murder
- one in nine arrests for a drug abuse violation
- one in four arrests for a weapons violation and for robbery.

2003 was actually the ninth year that there was a decline in juvenile arrests of this type. Two-thirds of juvenile punishments are handled through a juvenile **court** system. In some cases, juvenile punishments are handled through the adult court system. The adult **criminal** legal system is used more often in criminal cases where a young **offender** is closer to adulthood, or when more serious crimes have been committed.

Yarmouth, United Kingdom, 1736

The case of Elizabeth Thompson, aged fifteen – hanged for murder.

At the gallows she was told to confess her crime; but she refused. The jailer tied her arms, and the Executioner put the halter about her neck. She called, "Am I to be butchered to death?" The cap was pulled over her face, and immediately she called out, "Let me jump, let me jump". She fell to her death.

– Daily Gazetteer, 22 June, 1736

Glossary

abuse to hurt or injure through ill treatment

antisocial bad for society and causing annoyance to others

asylum place of safety

bandit robber or murderer who was often a member of a gang

convict find or prove a person is guilty; a person who has been convicted of a crime

court group of people before whom legal cases are heard

criminal anyone who breaks the law

curfew law requiring certain, or all, people to be off the streets at a stated time

cyber crime any crime using computers

death penalty punishment by death

detention punishment of being kept inside a secure place

deter discourage someone acting in a particular way

discipline system of strict rules to control behaviour

electronic tag device attached to someone that sends a signal to show where they are

enlist get someone to join in, or get their support

executed be put to death for a crime

famine extreme lack of food, with many people dying of hunger

FBI United State's Federal Bureau of Investigation, which investigates serious crime

flogged beaten severely with a rod or whip

forge make copies of items and pretend they are the real thing

gallows wooden structure used for hanging a person

hack gain access to a computer illegally

hanging practice of killing criminals by hanging them with a rope around the neck

hard labour heavy manual work as a punishment

immigrant someone who comes to live permanently in a foreign country

inmate person kept in prison

innocent free from guilt or blame

jury group of people in a court that decides if someone is guilty or not

justice administration of the law

juvenile young person who is not quite an adult

loiter stand around with the intent to commit an offence

migrate move from one area to settle in another

offender person who commits a crime

orphan young person whose parents are dead

patrol watch over an area

poach illegally hunt or catch animals on private property

prey person who is helpless, or unable to escape attack

probation period of time when a prisoner is released, but his or her behaviour is supervised

prosecute accuse a person of a crime in a court of law

reform correct or improve behaviour or habits

reformatory place similar to a prison, where the aim is to change the bad behaviour of young criminals

refuge place that provides shelter or protection

rural belonging to the countryside

sentence punishment set by a court

sheriff official of an area who is in charge of enforcing the law

slaughterhouse place where animals are slaughtered for food

slum city area of dirty run-down housing, and poor living conditions

suspect person who is thought to have committed a crime

transportation sending criminals far away to another country

trial hearing and judgment of a case in court

volunteer someone who offers to do a job without being paid

Index